Faralli

PREHISTORIC ROCK PICTURES
IN EUROPE AND AFRICA

FROM MATERIAL IN THE ARCHIVES OF THE RESEARCH INSTITUTE

FOR THE MORPHOLOGY OF CIVILIZATION · FRANKFORT-ON-MAIN

BY PROFESSOR LEO FROBENIUS AND DOUGLAS C. FOX

THE MUSEUM OF MODERN ART · NEW YORK

TABLE OF CONTENTS

PREFACE AND ACKNOWLEDGMENT

THAT an institution devoted to the most recent in art should concern itself with the most ancient may seem something of a paradox, but the art of the 20th century has already come under the influence of the great tradition of prehistoric mural art which began around the 200th century B.C. The formal elegance of the Altamira bison; the grandeur of outline in the Norwegian rock engravings of bear, elk and whale; the cornucopian fecundity of Rhodesian animal landscapes; the kinetic fury of the East Spanish huntsmen; the spontaneous ease with which the South African draftsmen mastered the difficult silhouettes of moving creatures: these are achievements which living artists and many others who are interested in living art have admired.

Such technical and esthetic qualities are enviable but no more so than the unquestioned sense of social usefulness which these prehistoric pictures suggest. Until recently our own mural art was usually an architect's after-thought, a mere decorative postscript. Now, under the Government art projects, it has seemed at times an artificial adjustment to the artist's economic needs rather than the result of any very urgent communal necessity (beyond the preservation of society's self-respect which might suffer if the artist starved). The mural art of the Spanish caves and African cliffs was, on the contrary, an integral and essential function of life, for these *painted* animals were almost certainly magic symbols used to insure the successful hunting of the *real* animals. Today walls are painted so that the artist may eat, but in prehistoric times walls were painted so that the community might eat.

We can, as modern men, no longer believe in the magic efficacy of these rock paintings; but there is about them a deeper and more general magic quite beyond their beauty as works of art or their value as anthropological documents. Even in facsimile they evoke an atmosphere of antediluvian first things, a strenuous Eden where Adam drew the animals before he named them. It is even possible that among them are man's earliest pictures. In any case, this is the way he drew and painted, apparently following continuous traditions for thousands of years in parts of the earth as remote from each other as the North Cape of Norway and the Cape of Good Hope.

The facsimiles and photographs reproduced in this book and shown in the exhibition are a small selection of material from a remarkable group of collections in Frankfort-on-Main. Assembled under the direction of Professor Leo Frobenius, they comprise the Prehistoric Rock Picture Gallery, which contains over three thousand facsimiles, and the Africa Archives, which include an ethnographic collection and the *Excerptur*, a great file of ten thousand drawings, two thousand color plates, two hundred manuscript volumes and over one hundred thousand reference cards indexing the characteristics, material and spiritual, of human culture.

These collections are administered by the Research Institute for the Morphology of Civilization (Forschungsinstitut für Kulturmorphologie) founded by Professor Frobenius in 1923. The field work of the Institute is carried on by the D. I. A. F. E., the German Inner-African Research Expedition. Founded by Professor Frobenius in 1904, it has carried out twelve major and several minor expeditions, not only to Africa but to important prehistoric centers in Europe and the Near East. The facsimiles in the present exhibition have been prepared by the artist members of the D. I. A. F. E., and, since they are duplicates, it is possible that they might find a permanent home in America. As the sizes of the facsimiles were not available for the catalog section, it is interesting to note here that they range from a few inches in size to about twenty-five feet, reproducing, with a few exceptions, the exact dimensions of the originals.

The Museum of Modern Art wishes to thank: Professor Frobenius, for his interest in the American exhibition; his American assistant, Douglas C. Fox, who has most generously given his time to plan and supervise the exhibition and prepare the text of the catalog; Miss Iris Barry, Curator of The Museum of Modern Art Film Library, who first suggested the exhibition to the Museum and carried on preliminary negotiations; and Walter P. Chrysler, Jr., for his interest and assistance.

ALFRED H. BARR, JR.

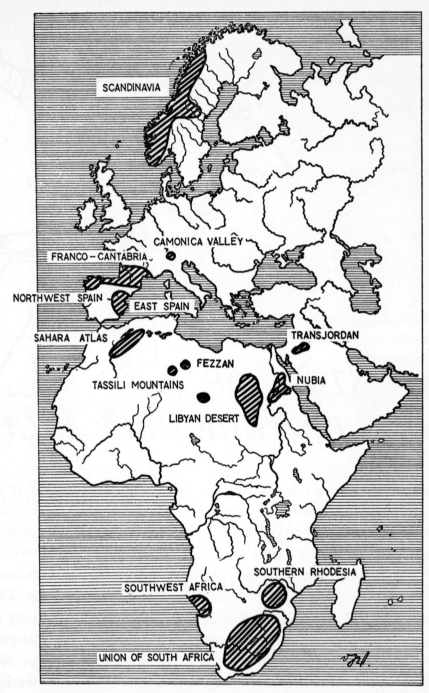

Rock picture districts in Europe and Africa

THE STORY OF
ROCK PICTURE RESEARCH

THE YEAR 1895 was a decisive one for the modern conception of
the early periods of human culture, for it was then that the French
scholar Rivière showed that in a cave of Northern Spain, discovered
sixteen years before by Baron Sautuola, there existed pictures which
had been painted in the Ice Age. The impression which this evidence
of Rivière's made on European science was a very curious one. The
matter was discussed at a meeting of the Anthropological Society in
Berlin, a body to which all the important scholars of the day belonged,
and a letter was read which described the Altamira paintings. According to this document, the paintings were neither primitive nor
simple, nor were they to be compared in any way with the daubs of

13

even the most gifted children—no, these pictures were true and great works of art. The letter went on to show that there was uncertainty as to how this discovery should be accepted. For it must be remembered that the pictures had been painted many thousands of years before the beginning of history, that they showed that Ice Age man had reached a level in matters of art so high as to be removed not so very far from our own, and, finally, that such evidence was in no sense compatible with the precepts of the then current evolutionary conception of the development of human culture. The letter was from the great French scholar, E. Cartailhac.

The gentlemen of the Anthropological Society gathered in Professor Bastian's room that evening shook their respective heads and said that there was no need to take the matter tragically. They would have to have further proofs, the proofs would have to be investigated and that would take time. In other words the skepticism typical of the erudition of the day tended to shelve a question which it would have been uncomfortable to face. In truth, however, this new discovery buzzed through many heads and the less it was spoken about the more it was thought of until it became a burden hard to cast off.

Why? Because, at that time, the West European intellect had come more and more to the conviction that the culture of the day was the highest to which man had ever attained . . . because it had dedicated itself more and more to the belief that the earlier and older cultures, though they might have enjoyed a certain stature and significance in ancient Greece, were in no sense to be compared with the greatness of a modern scientific existence . . . above all, because it was convinced that everything which had developed before the beginning of history (even then set at 3000 B. C.) could be regarded only as primitive, amateurish and insignificant in comparison with nineteenth century splendor.

Thus the establishment of the fact that man had possessed a splendid culture and a magnificent art thousands of years prior to our era was, shall we say, distinctly irritating.

14

Irritating—yes, painful, and because it was painful it was suppressed.

Whether there were many who were moved by other than the painful aspects of the case, it would be hard to say today. But at any rate there was one individual in whom the whole affair had started a train of thought which led in quite a different direction. It was, for instance, generally accepted that the older Stone Age culture, since it showed little relation to those of the post-glacial period, had died out when the ice receded northward. This older culture had borne testimony to the forceful grandeur of the age. Its art depicted the mammoth and the reindeer, the cave bear, bison, elk, wild horse and rhinoceros. After the Ice Age these animals, together with the implements, weapons and other attributes of this same culture, disappeared, vanished without a trace. German scholars thought that the culture had decayed and died. Not so the then youthful Leo Frobenius. It did not seem likely to him that anything so essentially alive could vanish so completely. Had it not died, its descendants would have to be sought elsewhere; had it really died, some traces of its cultural increment were bound to have cropped up in the cultures of a later period.

The young man—and he was very bold for the time—asked himself if it were not possible for this culture to have been indigenous to Africa as well as to Europe. He took into consideration the fact, then already known to science, that North Africa had not always been a desert, but rather that it had enjoyed a pluvial period at the very time when glaciers still covered the southern slopes of the Pyrenees. During this period its mountains must have been decked with trees, its valleys traced with a network of rivers, lakes and streams, and inland, southward from the coast, wide plains must have been the most characteristic feature of its landscape. Further, it was thought that the Straits of Gibraltar had not existed at that time, that the Mediterranean had been a lake and that Spain had been just as much a part of Africa as a part of Europe. Therefore, why should not the culture of the period have flourished in Africa as well as in Spain? Were that the case, then one could imagine that when the water evaporated and the plains turned into a desert, the African branch of this culture, if one wished to call it that, had moved ever southward towards the moist interior, that it had penetrated as far even as South Africa. Were this, too, the case, then—and at the thought of it the young man caught his breath—then this culture still could be alive *today*, still could be observed, grasped, studied and understood *today!*

It was a tremendous thought which came to a climax with the reflection that the Bushmen of South Africa today actually still paint pictures on the rocks. Travelers, from old Levaillant onwards, who had seen these paintings, had described them as more or less primitive daubs. But there was still the question to be faced of whether or not these daubs could be a last remainder, degenerate to be sure, but still a remainder of a culture which had flourished once in Spain.

That was the first reflection.

This reflection was coupled with an outspoken mistrust of certain so-called scientific premises of the day and in particular of the ruling theories in regard to the history and being of past—which was to say primitive—cultures. At that time two great German scholars were struggling for the palm. One was Adolf Bastian who preached that cultures rose in geographical independence, but that their growth lay in a definitely prescribed course of thought and feeling inherent in every member of the human race, something which he based on the assumption that all cultures were fundamentally alike. The second was Friedrich Ratzel, less intense but more methodical, who saw the source of the development of culture first in heredity and then in a series of contacts which resulted in A's borrowing or taking over the cultural attributes of B. Neither of these theories was sufficient for someone possessed by the idea of culture *per se*, as a totality, as a whole. Among Adolf Bastian's papers there lies a series of letters and proposals in young Leo Frobenius' handwriting, proposals in which the following train of thought was developed:

1. The most difficult obstacle to our understanding of culture is our

16

ignorance. We do not know enough. Any trained zoologist, given the leg of a beetle, can tell you the name of the bug it belongs to, and no botanist supposes that roses bloom on oak trees. We are familiar with the characteristics of the chemical elements, know how they can be combined, and that in combination they again have different characteristics. We even know what these characteristics are. But what do we know about culture? Nothing. Because we are lazy, phlegmatic and stupid, because we plume ourselves if we can string five or ten citations together to write a witty, anecdotal paper.

2. What do we need, then? Work! And more work! Every fact, object and belief which can help us to understand the growth of human culture should be recorded and indexed for use. It is a pure question of application, first to get the material together and then to see how much we can learn alone from the geographic distribution of certain culture elements (*i.e.* drum, bow, spear).

3. We will find that there are peoples of whom we do not know enough, and so it will be necessary to send out expeditions to find and gather the material we lack.

4. It will be our task to handle our material not only linguistically, descriptively and philologically but also graphically. That means that every expedition will be equipped with a staff of artists who will transfer to paper and canvas that which cannot be recorded accurately with the camera.

5. That is to say, one of the main tasks of a future serious "science of culture" and of a true culture-morphology will be to establish institutions for research and to send out expeditions.

Naturally, the answer to such proposals was negative. We lived then in another age, a period of arrogance and darkness, and the young man who made these suggestions was, in a more or less friendly fashion, shoved aside.

Still, the work has been done. It was carried out in accordance with a carefully considered plan for which long years of study have paved the way. We began with a series of questionnaires which were sent to various governments for distribution throughout certain parts of Africa and which won us a number of collaborators in the French, English and Belgian colonies. Then we created an organization which, as the German Inner-African Research Expedition (D. I. A. F. E.), was dedicated solely to the cultural investigation of that continent. We planned on twelve separate year-long undertakings with a year of rest in Europe between each. It was necessary to investigate first the living cultures in order to determine to what extent the original (not to be confused with the later so-called "historical") *Kulturkreislehre* (doctrine of culture circles) was valid.

The desk work of the last decade had shown that Africa was the continent most suitable for such an investigation. It began, in the manner indicated, in 1904. By 1912 we had come far enough to be able to devote more time to prehistoric material. In 1910 I had consulted at great length with Professors Flammand and Gautier, the greatest French prehistorians in the North African field, and by 1913 we were in a position to study and copy the prehistoric rock pictures of the Sahara Atlas region. In the same connection there followed in 1926 the investigation of the Nubian Desert, in 1928-30 the South African expedition, in 1932 the undertaking in Fezzan, in 1933 the first expedition in the Libyan Desert, and in 1934-35 the twelfth and last DIAFE which did comparative work throughout the desert belt, beginning in Transjordan.

As a result of these undertakings, in the course of which, as I may have indicated, there was a steady alternation from field to desk and from desk to field, there arose the Afrika Archiv, today the property of the city of Frankfurt-am-Main, the prehistoric Reichsfelsbildergalerie, of which this exhibition is a small part, and the Forschungsinstitut für Kulturmorphologie.

Neither the study nor the reproduction of prehistoric rock pictures is easy. If the rock surface were smooth and all on one plane, if the

18

lighting were regular and of the necessary strength and texture, if the colors and incisions were clear cut and not criss-crossed and pocked by erosion, then "perhaps" one would need only to avail oneself of a camera. But only "perhaps." For a lens cannot differentiate between that which is essential and that which is not. The result is that it is extremely difficult if not impossible to obtain an accurate conception of a rock picture from a photograph.

So there is nothing left but to have the pictures copied by hand, something which is not easy and which can be done satisfactorily only by those who have, so to speak, immersed themselves in the material and are sensitive to the spirit and mentality of an age which has passed. This will be hard for some people to understand. But the fact remains that every picture, whether carved into the rock by prehistoric man, drawn by a child or painted by a Raphael, is alive with a certain definite spirit, a spirit with which the facsimile must be infused.

There are two schools of thought and action with regard to the manner in which these pictures, most of them weather-worn and no longer intact, are to be reproduced. The one is purely scientific. It reconstructs. It considers the effects of erosion and, by eliminating them, seeks to reproduce what it believes was the original picture. The second paints what is there. It knows it is copying not merely a picture but a document in stone, a cultural document of which the chips, cracks and weathering are an historical part. This second school is that of the DIAFE. Everyone will agree that there is as much to be said for the one as for the other. But, for the very reason that our collections are documents of fallen grandeur, I insist that we keep on working in accordance with this principle. And in the course of time we have developed our own school with its own tradition, a school which, more and more, is learning to master the technical difficulties which confront it, a school of whose members I am inordinately proud.

Modern prehistory was born in France. French scholars, schooled by the finds in the north of that country and in Belgium, with the magnificent caves of the Dordogne and Arriège, so to speak, in their garden, have worked with a praiseworthy intensity and a fine fixity of purpose to build up the outline of its chronological structure. Perhaps "sequential" structure would be a better word, since we cannot yet be very sure of dates. This begins with the Old Stone Age (the Paleolithic: Chellean to Magdalenian) and goes through the Middle Stone Age (the Mesolithic: Azilian, Tardenoisean and early Campignian, etc.) into the New Stone Age (the Neolithic: beginning around 4000 B. C.).

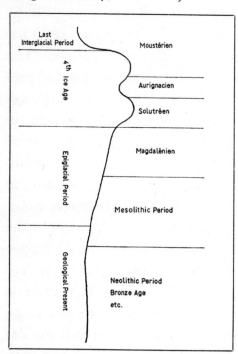

The Diluvial Period consists of four Ice Ages interspersed with three warmer periods or Interglacials. According to the results of the most recent geological and paleontological research, man appeared in Europe during the first Interglacial, that is, many hundreds of thousands of years ago, something which is indicated by the presence of certain stone artifacts in early diluvial strata. In the course of time he developed a series of what we call stone industries (Prechellean, Chellean, Acheulean, Cromerian, Clactonian, Levalloisian, Premousterian, Mousterian, etc.) which are named after the places where their respective products were first found. Prehistoric art had its beginning, as far as we know, in the last Ice Age, archaeologically in the Later Paleolithic.

This last Ice Age had two cold high points each of which, if one may mix metaphors, must have had a long duration. When we consider the centuries necessary for the development of the huge system

20

of glaciers with which it covered Europe, we must assume that it lasted for at least 30,000 years.[1] It has been established that the Mousterian culture, for instance, lies in the first high point, the Aurignacian, to which the earliest rock pictures belong, in the somewhat warmer period between the two peaks, and the Solutrean in the second high point. According to the lowest figures available, those of the noted Swedish geologist de Geer (who has recently made some remarkable investigations in America), the last phase of this last Ice Age, that is, from the second high point to the time when the glaciers had melted and gone, lasted from approximately 18,000 to 5000 B. C. In this period lie the Magdalenian, the Mesolithic (carrying on the New Paleolithic tradition) and the proto-Neolithic cultures. The Magdalenian, which produced the finest specimens we have of pre-historic art, probably flourished till 10,000 B. C. This is a high age to attribute to a culture which produced such magnificent and, in some cases, such finely preserved paintings and engravings. One of the many facts which speak for it, however, are the arctic (Scandinavian) rock pictures of a younger culture which, again, according to the geologists, must have existed at least as far back as 8000 B. C.

The paleolithic connection with Africa has been established by the discovery in Europe of the bones of African fauna such as the hippopotamus and the elephant in conjunction with early Old Stone Age implements. According to Vignard, Sandford and others, there is nothing to prevent us from assuming that man appeared in Europe and Africa simultaneously, and it has been established that the development of the early Old Stone Age culture was the same on both continents, something which justifies the application to North Africa and Egypt of the French classifications for the early paleolithic culture stages.

A question with which we are often faced is: "What do the pictures mean?" Now it is a fact that the European pictures have, on the sur-

[1] This figure and the ones which follow are based on geological findings. Although they are the lowest we have to go by, they are fantastically high from the culture-morphological standpoint.

face, very little to say. No one lives who can tell about their origin, and were it not for the thought which gave rise to the search for their like in Africa, their silence might well have been eternal. At the beginning my hope was so small that I could hardly have backed it with a positive: "I am sure." But, since then, our rich experience has enabled us to say: *"That which existed once in Europe lives on among its epigones in Africa today."*

In the Homburi Mountains in the Sudan, Desplagnes found rock pictures which were made by novices in the course of their initiation rites, something which we ourselves were able later to investigate further. Southward, this time in the forest of Liberia, Dr. German found more novice paintings which, since there were no rocks, had been made on mud walls erected for the purpose. In 1905 we obtained further evidence from a Congo race, hunting tribes, later famous as the "pygmies," which had been driven from the plateau to the refuge of the Congo. We met them in the jungle district between Kassai and Luebo. Several of their members, three men and a woman, guided the expedition for almost a week and were soon on friendly terms with us. One afternoon, finding our larder rather depleted, I asked one of them to shoot me an antelope, surely an easy job for such an expert hunter. He and his fellows looked at me in astonishment and then burst out with the answer that, yes, they'd do it gladly, but that it was naturally out of the question for that day since no preparations had been made. After a long palaver they declared themselves ready to make these at sunrise. Then they went off as though searching for a good site and finally settled on a high place on a nearby hill.

As I was eager to learn what their preparations consisted of, I left camp before dawn and crept through the bush to the open place which they had sought out the night before. The pygmies appeared in the twilight, the woman with them. The men crouched on the ground, plucked a small square free of weeds and smoothed it over with their hands. One of them then drew something in the cleared space with his forefinger, while his companions murmured some kind of formula

22

or incantation. Then a waiting silence. The sun rose on the horizon. One of the men, an arrow on his bowstring, took his place beside the square. A few minutes later the rays of the sun fell on the drawing at his feet. In that same second the woman stretched out her arms to the sun, shouting words I did not understand, the man shot his arrow and the woman cried out again. Then the three men bounded off through the bush while the woman stood for a few minutes and then went slowly towards our camp. As she disappeared I came forward and, looking down at the smoothed square of sand, saw the drawing of an antelope four hands long. From the antelope's neck protruded the pygmy's arrow.

I went back for my camera intending to photograph the drawing before the men returned. But the woman, when she saw what I was up to, made such a fuss that I desisted. We broke camp and continued our march. The drawing remained unphotographed. That afternoon the hunters appeared with a fine "buschbock," an arrow in its throat. They delivered their booty and then went off to the hill we had left behind us, carrying a fistful of the antelope's hair and a gourd full of its blood. Two days passed before they caught up with us again. Then, in the evening, as we were drinking a foamy palm wine, the oldest of the three men—I had turned to him because he seemed to have more confidence in me than the others—told me that he and his companions had returned to the scene of their preparations for the hunt in order to daub the picture with the slain antelope's hair and blood, to withdraw the arrow and then to wipe the whole business away. The meaning of the formula was not clear, but I did gather that, had they not done as they did, the blood of the dead antelope would have destroyed them. The "wiping out," too, had to take place at sunrise. The man begged me not to tell the woman that he had mentioned the matter. He seemed to have the greatest fear of the consequences of his talking, for on the next day he disappeared, his fellows with him.

Later, in South Africa, we found a connection between rock pic-

23

tures and mythological tradition, local mythology often explaining the rock paintings we found near ancient graves, something which the inquiring reader may find more about in *Erythräa*.[1]

The work of the Institute and of the expeditions has, however, led to results which go beyond the individual significance of these rock pictures. For instance, whoever studies the French and Spanish pictures will soon notice the presence of two completely different styles.

1. The first, which is generally called the *francocantabrian*, is best preserved in Southern France and Northern Spain. The pictures are in underground caves and usually portray large wild animals, most of which are shown at rest, that is, standing, or, as is the case with some of the bison on the ceiling of Altamira, even lying down. The representation of the human figure scarcely ever occurs. The pictures consist of engravings and exceedingly skillful polychrome paintings.

2. The second we call the *levant* or East Spanish style. The pictures are usually found in natural niches in the cliffs or under overhanging rocks, are exposed to the light of day and are usually monochromes carried out in red ochre. Occasionally they portray wild animals, but their main subject is man: man hunting, fighting, dancing or even climbing a tree. They emphasize not only a feeling for composition but a very live conception of movement, haste and speed—in direct contrast to the general immobility of the francocantabrian paintings and engravings.

Looking at both styles side by side, it is hard to believe that they are contemporaneous. Still, this is the case, however astonishing it may be that two such completely different mentalities flourished as neighbors for thousands of years. The evidence is there, and in this connection it is a pleasure to quote from a letter by our friend Professor Hugo Obermaier, of Madrid, in which he reports on a find which brought him the final proof of it. The letter concerns the Parpallo cave in Valencia.

[1] Leo Frobenius, *Erythräa*, Atlantis Verlag, Berlin and Zurich, 1931.

Professor Obermaier writes: "This cave, though there are no paintings on its walls, delivered us a thoroughly instructive stratography.

"a.) In the upper four metres of archaeological strata were found a middle and older Magdalenian, the latter with a few paintings and many engravings on loose slabs of rock, largely in the Cantabrian style but partly in the East Spanish style as well.

"b.) Below it lay, between four and five metres, a Solutrean ensemble with many paintings (and engravings) which could be recognized as twin phenomena to the 'levant-art,' a fact also emphasized by Breuil.

"c.) Between six and eight metres: Aurignacian.

"Thus the Parpallo cave becomes an extraordinarily important station, showing, as it does, that the influence of northern (Cantabrian) art reached far down along the east coast toward Southern Spain where years ago Breuil and I were able to establish francocantabrian elements in the wall paintings of the Pileta cave (Malaga).

"At the same time the levant zone developed its own art: the peculiar paintings of the 'Eastern Style.'

"For years there has been no doubt about the diluvial age of these paintings—but it is nevertheless not unimportant that finally animal paintings have been found in the archaeologically dateable strata of what were once dwelling places and particularly in those strata which are older than the Magdalenian.

"The Parpallo cave is not published yet and, for the time being, I can tell you only a little. But this you can use without any reservations whatever, for it is based on a very careful examination of the finds by both Professor H. Breuil and myself."

This letter of Obermaier's puts all further doubt aside and we now have a phenomenon before us for which we can produce ethnological as well as archaeological parallels. I can think of two types of pottery, absolutely individual in style, produced by the inhabitants of adjacent harbors in ancient Crete. The same thing occurred in New Guinea, an island where the ornament forms to be found in almost

25

Bison. Altamira, North Spain. FRANCOCANTA-
BRIAN STYLE.

Bowman. Saltadora, East Spain.
EAST SPANISH STYLE.

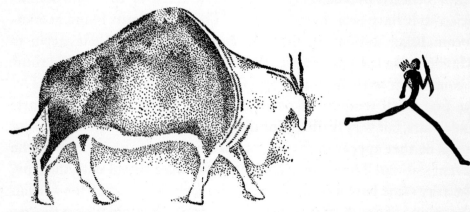

Eland. Khotsa Cave, Basutoland, South
Africa. FRANCOCANTABRIAN STYLE.

Bowman. Bogati Hill, Basutoland, South
Africa (reversed). EAST SPANISH STYLE.

every harbor were so distinctly individual that a connoisseur, even today, can determine the exact origin of any piece that is given him.

But these are trifles compared to the stupendous fact that these diluvial cultures, these cultures of the Ice Age, which lasted for thousands of years, existed side by side. We who have been fortunate enough to see and study the great rock picture galleries of Fezzan, the Libyan Desert and South Africa must try to understand what this means, for the same phenomenon, the same division into two contemporaneous styles which merge only in a much later period, exists

26

in Africa, too. It is amazing that, as far as style goes, it is practically impossible to tell the levant paintings (East Spanish) from those of the Libyan Desert. The same style appears again in Fezzan and crops up once more in South Africa, while in the Western Sahara there is a preference for the large animals (francocantabrian), still, heavy and at ease. This francocantabrian element, however, occurs in Fezzan and South Africa, too, and in Basutoland, for instance, we have both styles represented in the same picture (No. 145).

Let us look at the matter more closely. It is not the pictures alone which characterize the individuality of the two styles. It goes further. For instance, all the pictures of the levant style are to be found on or beneath overhanging rocks, while those of the francocantabrian style have been found in caves. The implements found at francocantabrian stations are Middle European (from Aurignacian to Magdalenian), while those at the East Spanish stations usually show a connection with Africa (Capsian). In the francocantabrian caves we find small weapons of ivory and bone, throwing sticks for darts and spears, but very little sign of the bow. On the other hand throwing sticks neither appear in the levant paintings nor do they occur at the levant stations. These East Spanish people were armed with the bow, the very same bow which we see in the rock paintings of the Libyan Desert and of South Africa. If we look about the world we see throwing sticks among the Eskimos, the Indians of Eastern America and the aborigines of Australia, that is, on the edge of the Oekumene. On the other hand the bow, which appears in the levant and the Libyan pictures, is *the* ancient weapon of the tropics.

Just as the one has been exiled to the farthest corners of the Arctic, Australia, America and South Africa (Kalahari Desert), so has the other been preserved in those tropical and semi-tropical regions where the destructive intervention of the younger, higher cultures has not yet become apparent. We also see that each weapon is characteristic of a separate mentality. The people with throwing sticks for their spears and darts, the dwellers in caves, cunningly use the com-

27

plicated relationships of their totemistic organizations and the whole paraphernalia of their symbolism to deceive themselves about the main issues of life. The users of the bow are of quite another stamp. Without illusion, they attack and destroy each other and are as aggressive as the former are defensive. Theirs is a cannibal-like mind, bent on conquest.

It is interesting to see, the more we go into the matter, how the contrasts appear, how the picture of "that which was" comes into focus, and how the cultural phenomena of an earlier period are revealed. In this short space it is not possible to do more than point in a direction. But anyone who has followed carefully the variations in style from prehistoric into archaeological and finally into historic times will see the main lines and know how necessary it is to use a special gauge for his comparisons rather than the scale with which he measures the more familiar occurrences of his daily life. For it has come to pass that we modern Europeans, concentrating on the newspaper and on that which happens from one day to the next, have lost the ability to think in large dimensions. We need a change of *Lebensgefühl*, of our feeling for life. And it is my hope that the enormous perspective of human growth and existence which has been opened to us by these pictures and by the researches of the modern prehistorian may serve to contribute in some small measure to its development.

LEO FROBENIUS

ROCK PICTURES
IN EUROPE AND AFRICA

SCANDINAVIA.   ON THE Norwegian coast of Northland
are monumental Stone Age rock pictures of elk, reindeer, whale, seal
and bear, drawn in natural size and depicted so accurately that they
are a joy to the eye even of a zoologist. These pictures are of recent discovery and are not so well known as the somewhat cruder South
Scandinavian Bronze Age engravings of ships, symbolic signs and
schematized human figures. They differ, too, from the Bronze Age
pictures not only in subject matter but also in technique. Their contours, instead of being cut or chiseled into the rock, show a smooth
surface which was probably achieved by polishing the stone with
wood and sand and water. These polished outlines have resisted the

This essay does not discuss rock pictures of the Nubian Desert and Transjordan.

erosion of ten thousand years better than the untreated granite surface so that they now stand in relief and produce an effect which
could not have been foreseen by their makers. In style they show a
certain relationship to the cave art of Western Europe, but it must

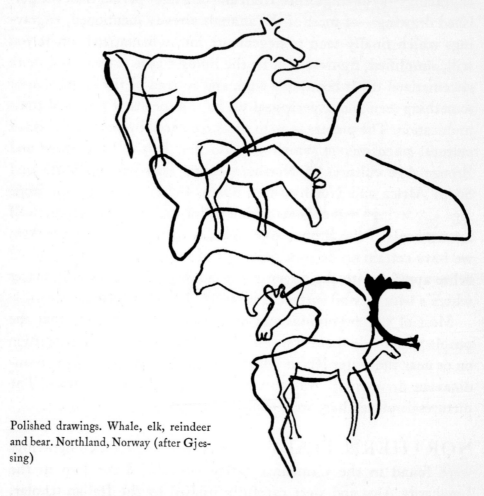

Polished drawings. Whale, elk, reindeer
and bear. Northland, Norway (after Gjes-
sing)

be born in mind, first, that this cave art is several thousand years
older and, second, that the early Scandinavian cultures are thought
to have developed in the north and then to have spread southward.
It is, however, by no means impossible that new discoveries will tend
to upset this theory and to show that a real connection with South-

western Europe, and consequently with Africa, existed in prehistoric times.

The Scandinavian Stone Age lasted from what beginnings we know not till approximately 2000 B. C. To it belong naturalistic engravings—as distinguished from and of a later period than the polished drawings—of most of the animals already mentioned, engravings which finally tend to degenerate into schematized, or, if you will, simplified, figures; that is: the living figure is more and more systematized till it becomes a sign, and instead of the expression of something seen and experienced we have a means of practical communication. The picture is, so to speak, replaced by writing. This is a cultural phenomenon which we also find in the later Stone and Bronze Age cultures of Northern Italy, Transjordan, North and South Africa and Northwestern Spain. Other Scandinavian Stone Age engravings depict boats which differ in contour from the well known boats of the Bronze Age. And, at the end of the Stone Age, we have certain crude rock paintings of human beings, done in red ochre applied with the finger and occurring in rock shelters, places where a natural wall surface is protected by an overhang.

Most of the engravings and drawings indicate merely that the people who made them were fishers and hunters, and their position on or near the water lets us hazard the guess that the historic Scandinavian drive-hunt[1] was also practiced in prehistoric times. The pictures displayed here were copied in 1934-35.

NORTHERN ITALY. A few years ago rock engravings were found in the Camonica Valley north of Lake Iseo in the Lombardy Alps and were carefully studied by the Italian scholar, G. Marro, who attributes them to the first Iron Age. In 1934-36 members of the Forschungsinstitut für Kulturmorphologie went into

---

[1] The trick was to drive the animals over a cliff into the water where men in boats would be waiting to dispatch them. In Southwestern Europe, where there are no fiords, animals were driven over precipices and killed by the force of the fall.

the district to copy these pictures and were fortunate enough to find a great many more which until that time were unknown. Most of the pictures represent hunting scenes: dogs chasing deer and followed by crudely drawn human figures, sometimes even by men ahorse, swinging their swords. Of particular interest are the frequently recurring pictures of pile dwellings with gable, cupola or barrel roofs. Similar structures with gable roofs often topped with phallic symbols are

Rock engraving. Man, stag and dog. Camonica Valley, North Italy

Rock engraving. Pile dwelling, rider, man with weapon and shield. Camonica Valley, North Italy

still built by the peasants of Asturias and Galicia in Northwestern Spain who use them as granaries.

In the Camonica Valley as in South Africa and in the francocantabrian caves the same rock surface was sometimes used by a series of artists. In such cases a layer of finer engravings, apparently belonging to an earlier period, appears beneath the rough contours of the surface compositions. These older layers also show animals, mostly deer, which are depicted much more naturally and competently (from our point of view) than those in the later pictures. The youngest pictures of all consist of geometric signs and symbols of which we seldom know the meaning. Professor Franz Altheim attributes all the Camonica Valley pictures to the Euganeans—according to Norden the original people of Italy—who show signs of contact with a North Pict culture.[1]

FRANCE AND SPAIN.

The cave of Altamira which lies above the picturesque patrician village of Santillana del Mar in the province of Santander may well be the cradle of Ice Age art in Western Europe. Twenty years after its chance discovery in 1876 archaeologists were able to show that the polychrome frescoes which covered the ceiling of its main gallery were not the work of shepherds and tramps, as the skeptics had supposed, but were the product of a culture which had flourished in paleolithic times during a period when the glaciers of the Ice Age still lay in a heavy and glittering mantle over Germany, France and Spain.[2]

In time more caves and rock shelters were found and excavated, and archaeological documents—artifacts of stone and bone, skeletons and pictures — were brought to light, fragments which have been pieced together to form a graphic, often incomplete, occasionally inaccurate but thoroughly fascinating mosaic of the life and times of prehistoric man.

The cave art was called francocantabrian to distinguish it from other forms of paleolithic art which were then and still are being discovered in Eastern Spain, Africa and the Near East. The Altamira[3] paintings owe their remarkable freshness to a landslide which probably occurred at the end of the last Ice Age and which sealed the cave hermetically till the end of the nineteenth century. The pictures

[1] The Euganeans, Professor Altheim tells me, used to live between the Alps and the sea but were driven into the mountains by the Illyrian Venetians around 900 B. C. The Camonica Valley is named after one of their tribes, the Camuni, and the neighboring Trompia Valley after another one of them, the Trumplini. Inscriptions have been found which probably indicate that these Euganeans were an Italian "ur-folk" (original race) and not an Indogermanic people. The rock pictures begin with the first Iron Age and continue into the Middle Ages.

[2] Altamira has been most thoroughly excavated and investigated by Professors Obermaier and Breuil, whose first work on it appeared in 1916. A revised edition, *The Cave of Altamira*, in French and English, was published in 1935.

[3] The facsimilies from the caves of Altamira, Castillo and La Pasiega we owe to the kindness of Professor Obermaier who obtained permission for us to work at these and other Spanish prehistoric stations.

begin with the Aurignacian,[1] go through the Solutrean and come to full flower in the Magdalenian. Their classification is, roughly, as follows:

Aurignacian: tectiforms, hand silhouettes, contour drawings and fragments outlined or blocked in with red, clay finger drawings and simple engravings.

Solutrean: tectiforms and line drawings in black, engravings of horses and hinds.

Magdalenian: a few paintings in black and the whole group of polychromes in their various stages of development.

One of the Castillo pictures (No. 30), the faded polychrome of a bison painted over the still faintly discernible silhouettes of several human hands, is thought to be a product of the Altamira school which is only some fifteen miles distant as the crow flies. Were it not for the landslide most of the Altamira polychromes would be just as faded as this Castillo bison.

Rock painting. Elephant. North Spain (after Breuil)

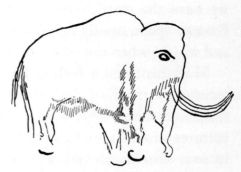

Rock engraving. Mammoth. South France (after Breuil)

The large polychrome of the bison from Font de Gaume (No. 25) is a good French example of the francocantabrian school as is the engraving of the cave bear from the adjacent grotto of Les Combarelles (No. 22).

In contrast to the francocantabrian pictures, almost all of which deal with animals in a more or less quiet pose, some even lying down,

[1] For the archaeological chronology see page 20.

34

Rock painting. Stag hunt. Eastern Spain (catalog no. 53)

we have the small, lively compositions from the rock shelters of Eastern Spain, mostly monochromes which deal with human beings and which, when they show animals at all, show them in action.

Movement and a feeling for composition are the main characteristics of the East Spanish or levant paintings. The levant and francocantabrian schools are contemporaneous, the products of two cultures which existed side by side for thousands of years, each with its own customs, its own weapons and its own *style*. The stone artifacts of the levant culture are African, those of the francocantabrian, Central European. The levant paintings are often hard to tell apart from those of the Libyan Desert. On the other hand, in Africa, we find elements of the francocantabrian schools in the monumental rock pictures of animals in the Sahara Atlas, while elements of both cultures are to be found in the engravings of Fezzan (Central North Africa) and the paintings of the South African Union.

In Northwestern Spain, in the province of Galicia, there are rock pictures which fit into neither the francocantabrian nor the levant categories and which occur not in rock shelters nor in caves but on granite boulders in the woods, on the moors and—when they have not been destroyed—in the fields. These are Bronze Age engravings of signs, schematized human and animal figures, "cups and rings" and their more highly developed offspring, the "labyrinths." Cups and rings consist of shallow hollows in the rocks in connection with or surrounded by concentric circles and are the products of a megalithic culture which once flourished in Brittany, the United Kingdom and Northern Europe. There have been and are other megalithic cultures in other parts of the world, but the cups and rings are, with a few exceptions, a European phenomenon. The more complicated of the spirals and concentric circles we call labyrinths because of the resemblance some of them bear to the labyrinth pattern on the coins of Cnossus from 200 to 60 B. C. But what they mean is still a mystery.[1] In finding and copying them in the summer of 1936 we were greatly assisted by Dr. Enrique Campo Sobrino, of Santiago de la Compostela, a Spanish scholar who has devoted many years to their investigation.[2]

SAHARA ATLAS. The fertile strip of the Algerian coast reaches inland approximately as far as Constantine. To the east of this old city are the great Schotts, the remains of earlier watersheds and consequent fertility; westward lie the rocky valleys and ravines of the Sahara Atlas. If we follow them toward Morocco we come, near Igli, to the Susfana Valley which runs northward and in which a greater part of the Sahara Atlas rock pictures are to be found.

[1] The Cretan labyrinth pattern occurs in a megalithic complex on the island of Weir, on the famous Etruscan Tragliatella vase, as a graffito on the walls of a house in Pompeii and again on the walls of a house in Pinal County, Arizona. Somewhat similar representations are to be found on Babylonian clay tablets portraying the entrails of sacrificial beasts and again on the wooden and stone churingas (where they designate totems) of the Aranda tribe in Central Australia. The latter cannot distinguish between concentric circles and a spiral, both of which mean for them a waterhole or "the home" of a particular totem.

[2] For the specialist, Dr. Sobrino's *Corpus Petroglyphorum Gallaeciae*, published by the Seminario de Estudios Gallegos, Santiago, 1935, will be of interest. The plates—photos from stone and reconstructions—are excellent.

These pictures were given serious attention some forty years ago by the geologist Flamand and the geographer Gautier, whom we must thank for the new vision they gave us of the geological and artistic past of the country. In 1913 the DIAFE VI with a staff of four painters set out for this region, first, to excavate prehistoric tumuli and dolmen and, second, to copy the much older rock pictures and so to lay the foundations of what has now become the prehistoric Reichsfelsbildergalerie with facsimiles of more than three thousand rock pictures from Africa and Europe. The work began in the neighborhood of Figig with the pictures of the Jaschu Plateau, continued southward to Taghit and later eastward to Afflu, el Richa and Djelfa. The results of the expedition dovetailed neatly with the conclusions of the French scholars and are contained in *Hadschra Maktuba*,[1] to which Professor Obermaier was kind enough to contribute a foreword.

"In the Sahara Atlas," writes Frobenius, "the enormous difference between the ur-historic (original) culture, no matter to what period it has still remained alive, and the rigid archaeological cultures coming from the Mediterranean is sharply apparent. The rock pictures of the latter are characterized by script signs, chariot wheels and other symbols and, above all, by their smallness. In contrast we have the splendid conception of the wild animals found in the monumental pictures of the *bubalus antiquus* (old buffalo) and of the elephant, a con-

Rock engraving. Two fighting buffaloes. Sahara Atlas, North Africa (catalog no. 87)

[1] Kurt Wolff Verlag, Munich, 1925.

37

ception which typifies the ur-historic culture. As a sort of middle stage between the two there are the somewhat smaller engravings of cattle in conjunction with human figures (especially in Tiout) which are very similar to those of Central Fezzan. In 1935 a branch of the DIAFE XII, which began in Transjordan and continued through the Libyan Desert, working westward under Fox, visited these stations again, thereby increasing our material, and a second division went southward from Biskra to study the pictures of the Wadi Itel which had already been made known by the French. Here Dr. Volhard and the painter, Marr, were able to make facsimiles which are among the most valuable in our collection."

FEZZAN.

FEZZAN. South of the former Turkish province of Tripolitania there flourished some 2000 years ago the ancient kingdom of the Garamantae which was visited and described by the Greek traveler Herodotus and was finally, at the beginning our era, destroyed by the Romans. The Romans are there again and now the name of Balbo, the military governor, has replaced that of Balbus under whom the triumph over the Garamantae was celebrated.

This region south of Tripolitania is known as Fezzan and was penetrated by British explorers as early as the beginning of the last century. Some eighty years ago Heinrich Barth, German member of a British expedition, found in a desolate valley rock pictures of cattle and of human figures with animal heads. He made sketches of them and showed these to Professor Movers, then the prime authority on such matters, who decided that the pictures were Phoenician, a conclusion in which Duvernier and others agreed. These sketches were lost, but on the strength of the notes which Barth left at his death Frobenius was able not only to rediscover the pictures which Barth had found, a facsimile of one of which is in this exhibition (No. 96), but to find a great many more in a region where none were thought to exist.[1]

[1] These pictures have been published by the Forschungsinstitut für Kulturmorphologie in the volume *Ekadi Ektab* (1937).

Fezzan is the land of the Tuareg and the Tedda who, till recently, have fought for centuries for the possession of the oases left over from the Garamantae period. During the War Frobenius was fortunate enough to encounter African prisoners from this region and to question them closely concerning it. They reported that in certain valleys there lived weird spirits which stared out from the rocks, transfixing the traveler with their gaze and turning him to stone—a belief which was confirmed later by natives from the Lake Chad region. One thing dovetailed with another so neatly that Frobenius was determined to investigate the matter further, a move which invited the skepticism of the scientific world and the derision of the Italian authorities in Africa. Mussolini, however, was interested and in 1932 the expedition (DIAFE X) started southward, one branch heading for Inner Fezzan and the stone plateau between Mursuk and Ubari and the other for Ghat and the Tassili Mountains.

In the deep ravines at the very center of the plateau Frobenius found no less than four main picture stations. He writes that here there were two types of pictures, one depicting wild animals, among them giraffes eighteen feet high, the other human figures sometimes with animal heads. The most frequently recurring animals were giraffe, *bubalus antiquus*, elephant, rhinoceros and crocodile (or waran). The style in which the human figures were depicted was apparently related on the one side to that of the levant art of Spain and on the other to that of early Egyptian art. There were, for instance, no less than four representations of the Egyptian god Bes.

In the second compositions (human figures), among them the Barth pictures, there often occurred the pictures of cattle which sometimes, Frobenius says, "bore disks between their horns, just as in Egypt. This reminded us that in the Sahara Atlas were pictures of rams with disks between their horns and that Georg Schweinfurth had already posed the question of whether or not these could be the ur-pictures of the Egyptian ram god, Jupiter Ammon."

A year later (DIAFE XI) Frobenius found in the Libyan Desert

rock paintings which were quite clearly those of the Egyptian god
Set, something which tended to confirm him in the belief, first suggested by Schweinfurth, that the ideas embodied in the figures of many
gods which we know as Egyptian came from the west, that these ideas
traveled slowly eastward across the wastes of what are now the Sahara

Rock engraving. Bull with symbolic
signs between the horns. Fezzan, North
Africa

and Libyan Deserts, which were then dry countries, as is South Africa,
but by no means so desolate as they are today, and that these ideas
were renovated and remodeled by the Egyptians, who finally gave
them the historical stamp with which we are familiar.

Since then Gautier and Reygasse have found in the Tassili Mountains rock pictures of war chariots in the Mycenean style and the
Italians have found in Fezzan pictures of chariots similar to those we
found in Transjordan in 1934, facts which indicate that this North
African rock picture art (engraving) must have lasted till quite a late
period.

The members of the DIAFE x who went into the Tassili Mountains found in caves and grottoes red-brown monochromes of camels
and other domestic animals, subjects which are still depicted occasionally by the Tuaregs and whose origin must be recent since there

were no camels (dromedaries) in Africa before the year 500 A. D. They also found older pictures of hunting scenes in which men and dogs, apparently forerunners of the Saluki, are depicted chasing Barbary sheep, pictures of men with animal heads, as in South Africa, and of women with short skirts, as in Eastern Spain.

LIBYAN DESERT.   It was not until after the World War when the automobile began to replace the camel as a means of transport that the territory between the Nile and the Italian colony of Libya south of the oases gradually began to appear in its proper outlines. This, the Libyan, the greatest and most terrible of all African deserts, was till recently, and to a certain extent still is, a blank spot on the map, a blank in which 9000 foot mountains, a 3000 foot plateau and a chain of sand dunes almost a thousand miles long—the Great Sand Sea—are beginning to appear. Most of our knowledge of it is inevitably bound up with the names of Rohlfs, King, Beadnell, Ball, Prince Kemal el Din, Hassanein-Bey, Bagnold, Clayton, Almasy and Shaw, men who with camel, caterpillar tractor, automobile and airplane were the first to undertake its exploration. When Frobenius set out from Kharga Oasis in 1933, rock paintings had already been found in the Uwenat Mountains. Our two expeditions, DIAFE XI and XII (1933-35), investigated these finds and, concentrating on prehistoric material, made many new ones. We stretched our work to cover the geographically known but prehistorically untouched border districts of the desert and so made what is perhaps the decisive contribution to the prehistoric exploration of this whole region. The Forschungsinstitut für Kulturmorphologie hopes to publish the first results of this work, compiled in detail by Dr. Hans Rhotert, in the summer or autumn of 1937.

The most important paintings are in Ain Dua at the southwestern base of the Uwenat Mountains about 370 kilometers southwest of Kufra. Others lie in the Khargur Tahl, a sandstone valley in the same range (which is mostly of granite), and still more in Wadi Sora which

41

lies 200 kilometers to the north on the southern hang of the Gilf Kebir Plateau. And then there are a few pictures in the Yerhauda Mountains, south of Uwenat. At Ain Dua the constant recurrence of pictures of cows with exaggerated udders would seem to indicate that their painters must have had a flourishing dairy and livestock industry, not with cattle such as we know but with a stag-like *bos* species, now extinct. Human beings armed with bow and arrow appear in compositions which, despite their lively movement, already show a degenerated formality. In the long stretches of the Khargur Tahl there

Rock engraving. Cow. Libyan Desert (South)

Rock engraving. Cow. Libyan Desert (North)

are as many engravings as there are paintings, some of the latter in miniature depicting domestic scenes which are often portrayed in the fullest detail. The richest paintings, however, are in the semi-cupolas, more overhangs than caves, of Wadi Sora. Here we have human figures in the most lively movement: bowmen in every possible position, acrobats, dancers, swimmers and people in costumes, one next to the other, and even the "handprints" which occur in the francocantabrian caves. Some of these pictures are so similar to those of Eastern Spain that Professor Obermaier holds the style of both to be practi-

Rock painting. A fight between animal-headed bowmen. Libyan Desert

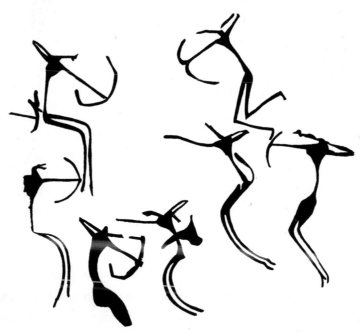

Rock painting. A fight between animal-headed bowmen; degenerate style with schematized figures. Libyan Desert

43

Left: Rock painting. Animal-headed human figure pierced with arrows. Libyan Desert (detail from catalog no. 69). Right: Egyptian representation of the god, Set.

cally identical. On the other hand there are also pictures which in subject (the jackal-headed god, Set) and treatment (exaggerated shoulders and narrow waist) indicate the possibility of a relationship with Egypt. The rich finds we made of stone artifacts of various types lead us to believe that these pictures were painted in the late Old Stone Age (Late or Upper Paleolithic). All these artifacts, as is usual in the desert, were found on the surface.

SOUTH AFRICA. In the rocky hills and mountains of Southern Rhodesia, Southwest Africa and the States of the South African Union, the so-called "Bushman paintings" are so numerous that one can almost count on finding them wherever an overhang protects a smooth rock surface from the weather. The name "Bushman paintings" would seem to indicate that the Bushmen, a small-statured folk with a "primitive"—a better word would be degenerate —culture who now live in the wastes of the Kalahari Desert, were responsible for their origin. Certainly many of the South African paintings and engravings have a connection with the Bushman culture, but on the other hand it is just as certain that many of them are the product of other and of much higher cultures than that of the present day Bushmen. To copy these pictures and to gather the legends connected with them was one of the main tasks which confronted the DIAFE IX of 1928-30.

44

Southern Rhodesia, which is bordered on the north by the Zambesi and on the south by the Limpopo, is, archaeologically, one of the most interesting of the South African provinces. Within its precincts are to be found the material remains of a high culture of which its present inhabitants know little or nothing. These remains consist of:

1. Stone buildings, the so-called "Zimbabwe" ruins named after the largest of their kind, the "Great Zimbabwe" near Fort Victoria.

2. Underground tin and copper mines which occur as far northward as the Belgian Congo and reach southward into the Transvaal.

3. Stone terraces which stretch over the highlands of Inyanga and cover every hill and mountain from top to bottom. We know of such terraces in other parts of the world where they are still in use. Here in Southern Rhodesia they have deteriorated with the years and are not planted by the natives.

4. Well built underground houses of stone, so-called "slave pits."

5. The rock paintings, which are here particularly numerous in the granite hills.

These paintings are not to be compared with those in other parts of South Africa, but are a type in themselves, a type closely related to the older culture elements of the territory. There is no doubt today that these culture elements, in turn, were closely related to the early cultures of Western Asia (Sumeria and Elam) and with the Negada culture in Egypt. That is to say: the Southern Rhodesian culture of which the rock paintings are a product must have flourished between 4000 and 3000 B. C.[1]

The Southern Rhodesian rock pictures are painted in red iron oxide which is occasionally flecked with white, a color which does not stand up too well against the weather. They differ from the other South African pictures in content as well as style. To be sure, hunting scenes do occur occasionally, but the portrayal of animals, though beautifully

[1] For more on this see Leo Frobenius, *Erythräa*, Atlantis Verlag, Berlin and Zurich, 1931.

done, nevertheless gives one the feeling that there is less emphasis on the beasts as such than there is on painting a surface-filling composition. In human representation the frontal position and the wedge-shaped trunk are so predominant that the casual beholder cannot but make a mental comparison with Egyptian paintings. The subject is confined chiefly to religious scenes (burials and rain ceremonies) and

Rock painting. Burial scene. Male corpse and two weeping women. Southern Rhodesia (catalog no. 120)

the illustration of myths about the evening star and the moon. The latter is personified on earth by the king, the ruler of that sacred state —still in existence when the Portuguese arrived—which will later order his destruction. Local legend, the only living relic of an ancient past, furnished the key to the meaning of many of the paintings.

For instance there is the myth which relates how the high priest had a vision in which he saw that the only way to end the drought would be to bury alive a virgin princess under a certain tree. There were no marriageable virgins available in the royal house, so he caught a young one and shut her up till she was of age. Then she was buried beneath the tree. Immediately the tree began to grow. It grew for three days and three nights and, as the morning star appeared at the end of the third night, the top of the tree touched the sky and the

46

morning star sent down the rain. This is the explanation of pictures No. 122 and No. 123. We see the priest standing before the dying princess who lies beneath the tree and in the sky we see Venus (Massassi), the morning star, sending down the rain. In No. 123 the tree is schematized and at its top is a serpent, even today a symbol for rain.

Rock painting. Rain ceremony. Southern Rhodesia (catalog no. 122)

Ritual regicide, which is believed to have taken place at astronomically determined intervals, was customary in the sacred state. Picture No. 127 depicts such a ceremony. On the right stands the king wearing the bull hide in which he will be buried. Further to the right the hide is rolled up with the king inside it and below it is a sacrifical animal with the blood streaming from its mouth. In the centre is the mountain in which the king will be buried. In the upper left corner we see the new king receiving a bow, symbol of life and power, while near him a sorrowful figure mourns the fate of his predecessor.

47

Rock painting. Burial scene. A lying figure (dead king?) wearing a mask, below it a smaller lying figure, also accompanying figures, probably priests. Southern Rhodesia (catalog no. 129)

Peculiar to Southern Rhodesia are the frequently recurring pictures of trees and plants, even of whole landscapes and of lakes with fish in them. In picture No. 121 we see a man about to descend into such a lake. He has thrown away his bow in indication of his determination to die. At the left we see a weeping woman sitting on a rock. This picture takes on meaning when we hear the legend about the king's son who wanted to marry his sister and who, when this was prohibited, went into the lake (Dsivoa) while his sister wept for him upon the shore.

There are other equally typical pictures for which we have no explanation. They show sausage or cigar-like forms standing neatly in rows. We call them formlings (see pictures No. 130 and 131). Per-

48

haps it may be that they portray the peculiar formations of the granite landscape or that the ones in which human figures occur reflect the belief, more current in the Near East, that man was born out of the rock or, in alluvial territories, was shaped in and of the earth. "I was made in secret and curiously wrought in the lowest parts of the earth." This ancient belief was not unknown to those cultures (Elam and Sumeria) to which the old Southern Rhodesian culture is believed to be related. The natives call all these pictures "Madsimu Dsangara": "the apparitions of the spirits of the forgotten dead."

SOUTH AFRICAN UNION

The rock pictures of the South African Union consist of both paintings and engravings. The former are usually polychrome, often painted in one layer over the other, and deal chiefly with hunting scenes but also with animal-headed human beings dancing, in procession and in council. The latter, which never occur where there are paintings, deal

Rock painting. Man with elephant head. Basutoland, South African Union (catalog no. 146)

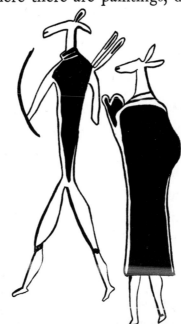

Rock painting. Two costumed animal-headed human figures. Orange Free State, South African Union

49

solely with animals and, with one exception, never portray more than one of these at a time. They are done on hard rock, dolerite or basalt, and favor the rhinoceros, the hippopotamus, the antelope and the giraffe. They are not very large and are seldom contour engravings as in the Sahara Atlas. In the main, the artist punches away the whole inner surface of his composition and does it so skillfully that often the pattern of the skin and the bony substructure of the animal he portrays are visible. From the technical standpoint some of these engravings are among the finest pictures we know of in the South African field. The stone artifacts which have been excavated near them

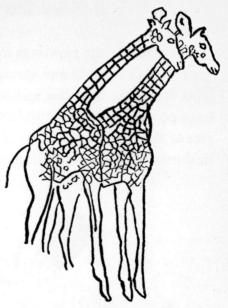

Rock engraving. Two giraffes. West Transvaal, South African Union

are of the Smithfield culture, the origin of which is obscure and in which North African neolithic as well as South African paleolithic elements are present. On the other hand archaeological material found in some of the rock shelters where paintings occur is definitely paleolithic.

SOUTHWEST AFRICA

The main rock picture district of Southwest Africa reaches from the Nau Gap, south of Rehobott, northward to Outjo near the Ovamba-land border. Here again there are both paintings and engravings. The latter, in the north of the district, depict animals, human and animal footprints and, more rarely, degenerate geometric signs. The human footprints are believed to indicate the direction of waterholes and the animal tracks to tell the hunter that he has entered the territory of such and such a tribe whose game he may not shoot and whose crops,

50

if any, he may not disturb. Infringement of this rule is punishable by death.

The polychrome paintings in the rock shelters in the South depict giraffe, ostrich, kudu and springbok, the monochromes usually show fable creatures, bowmen and men in processions. An exception is a large polychrome of men and animals (No. 147) in the Leopard Ravine of the Brandberg. This is a picture which has nothing to do with Bushman mentality or Bushman art. The richly costumed human fig-

Rock painting. Finely accoutred bowman. Southwest Africa (detail from catalog no. 156)

51

ures have weapons, clothing and a headdress which seem to be the product of an Egyptian-Assyrian culture and which move us to a comparison with the pictures of Southern Rhodesia, a comparison which does not tell us a great deal. How this one picture, obviously the product of a high culture, came to be painted in Bushman territory (for that is what it used to be) is a mystery for which we have no explanation.

DOUGLAS C. FOX

4 Polished rock drawing. Elk, reindeer, bear. Leikness, Norway

2 Polished rock drawing. Brown bear. Valle, Norway

9 Rock engraving. Animal and what are probably sacrificial axes. Vingen, Norway

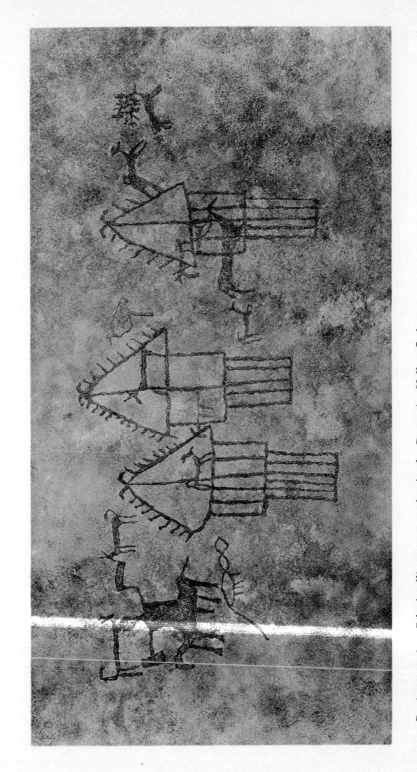

21 Rock engraving. Pile dwellings, men and animals. Camonica Valley, Italy

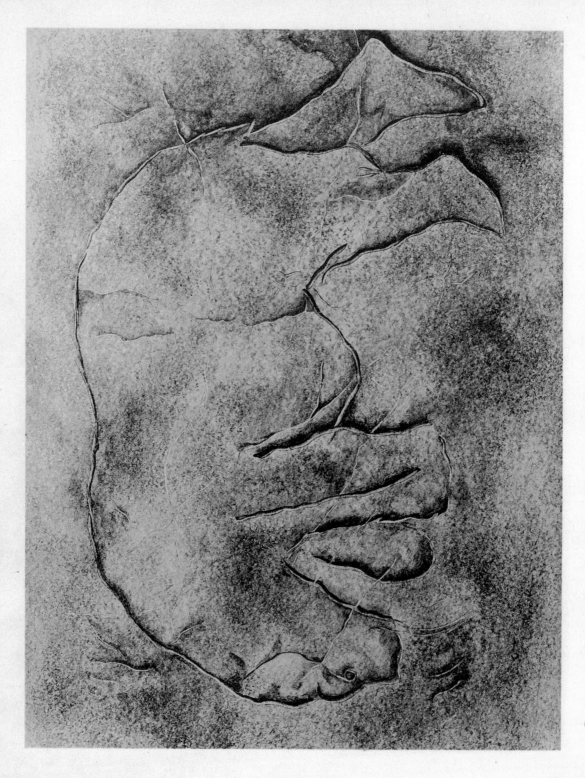

22 Rock engraving. Cave bear. Les Combarelles, Les Eyzies, Dordogne, France

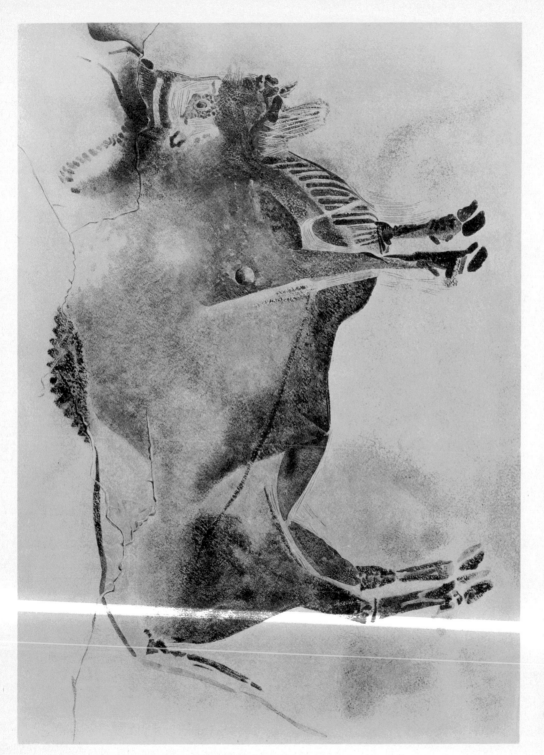

44 Polychrome painting, partly engraved. Bison cow. Altamira, Northern Spain

Rock painting (photograph of actual site). Two lying bison. Altamira, Northern Spain

Rock engraving. Labyrinths. Galicia, Northwestern Spain

79 Rock painting. A fight, apparently for possession of a bull. Khargur Tahl, Libyan Desert

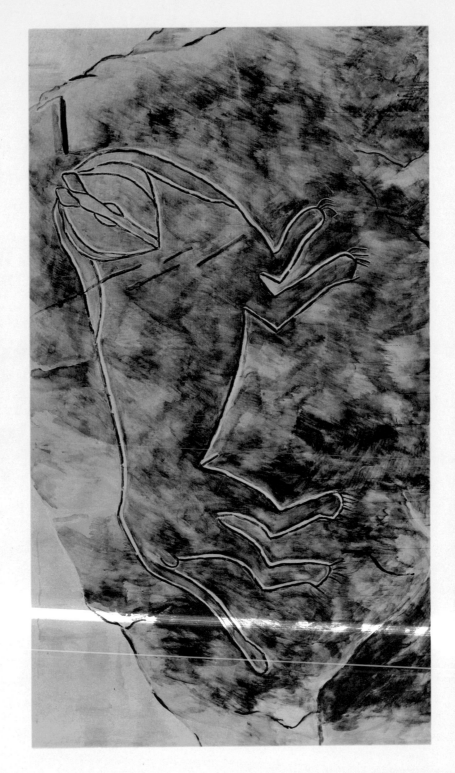

83 Rock engraving. Lion, en face. Jaschu Plateau. Sahara Atlas

107, 108, 115 Terrace with rock engravings. In Habeter, Fezzan

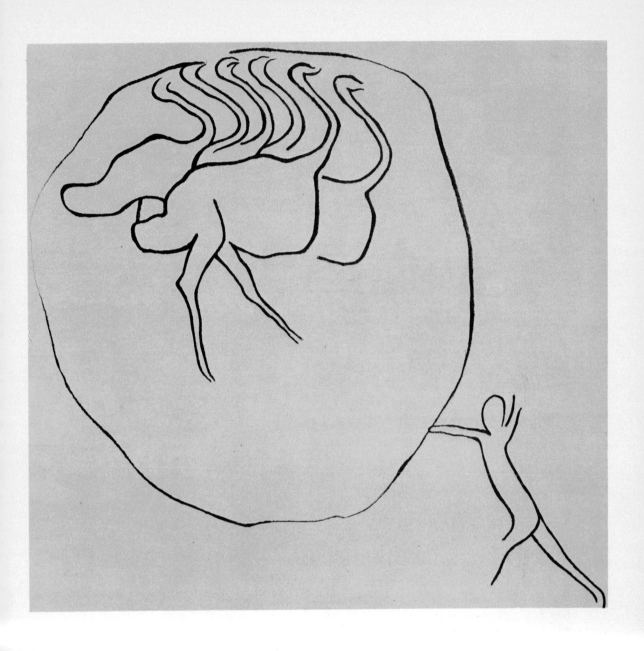

106 Rock engraving. Six ostriches in what is possibly the hunter's magic circle. In Habeter, Fezzan

133 Rock painting. Large elephants, quagga, antelopes, formlings and figures.
Mtoko Cave, Southern Rhodesia

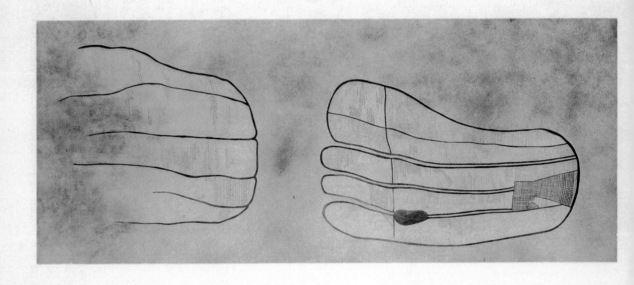

130 Rock painting. Group of large formlings. Makumba Cave, Chinamora Reserve, Southern Rhodesia

145 Rock painting. Large eland and human figures. Khotsa Cave, Basutoland, South African Union

157 Rock painting (photograph of actual site). Hunting scene. Naukluft, Southwest Africa

CATALOG OF FACSIMILES

SCANDINAVIA 1 Polished rock drawing, Glamfiord, Norway. Elk and reindeer.

*2 Polished rock drawing, Valle, Norway. Brown bear.

3 Polished rock drawing, Valle, Norway. Whale and seal.

*4 Polished rock drawing, Leikness, Norway. Two elk, two reindeer, two bears. *Site illustrated.*

5 Rock engraving, Drammen, Norway. Fish.

6 Rock engraving, Drammen, Norway. Whale.

7 Rock engraving, Rödöy, Norway. Hare on skis, a fable figure.

8 Rock engraving, Vingen, Norway. Deer-like animals with symbolic signs and schematized human figures.

*9 Rock engraving, Vingen, Norway. Animal and what are probably sacrificial axes.

10 Rock engraving, Tennes, Norway. Schematized human figure.

11 Finger painting, Trontveit, Telemark, Norway. Human figures.

12 Finger painting, Sandhalsan, Norway. Elk.

ITALY 13 Rock engraving, Cimbergo, Camonica Valley. Semi-geometric figure.

14 Rock engraving, Cimbergo, Camonica Valley. Bulls' heads.

15 Rock engraving, Cimbergo, Camonica Valley. Above, ibex with exaggerated horns; below, probably chamois, degenerate style.

Unless size is given, all facsimiles have been made in the size of the original.

ITALY

16 Rock engraving, Nacquane, Camonica Valley. Man with sword and shield spearing a fox.

17 Rock engraving, Nacquane, Camonica Valley. Men, deer and pile dwelling.

18 Rock engraving, Nacquane, Camonica Valley. Probably mountain goats.

19 Rock engraving, Nacquane, Camonica Valley. Runner.

20 Examples of the runner motif (swastika) found in various parts of the world.

*21 Rock engraving, Nacquane, Camonica Valley. Pile dwellings, men and animals.

FRANCE
Francocantabrian style

*22 Rock engraving, Les Combarelles, Les Eyzies, Dordogne. Cave bear.

23 Rock engraving, Les Combarelles, Les Eyzies, Dordogne. Mammoth.

24 Rock engraving, Les Combarelles, Les Eyzies, Dordogne. Anthropomorphic figure.

25 Polychrome painting, Font de Gaume, Les Eyzies, Dordogne. Bison.

26 Sculptured frieze of horses in Cap Blanc, a small open cave near Les Eyzies. This is the only sculptured frieze we know of in prehistoric art.

NORTHERN SPAIN
Francocantabrian style

27 Contour painting, Castillo, Puento Viesgo. Fragment of a bison.

28 Painting, Castillo, Puente Viesgo. Tectiform.

29 Painting, Castillo, Puente Viesgo. Scutiform signs.

30 Painting, Castillo, Puente Viesgo. Lying bison painted over the faintly visible silhouettes (from an earlier period) of hands and animals.

NORTHERN SPAIN Francocanta- brian style	31	Animal head, Castillo, Puente Viesgo. A natural stalagmite touched up here and there with black so as to represent a bison standing on its hind legs.
	32	Rock engraving, Castillo, Puente Viesgo. Ibex.
	33	Contour painting, La Pasiega, Puente Viesgo. Stag.
	34	Contour painting, La Pasiega, Puente Viesgo. Horse.
	35	Contour painting, La Pasiega, Puente Viesgo. Horse.
	36	Contour painting, La Pasiega, Puente Viesgo. Horse, bison, signs.
	37	Painting, La Pasiega, Puente Viesgo. Bison and horse.
	38	Contour painting, La Pasiega, Puente Viesgo. Bison with a spear (?) in its back.
	39	Rock engraving, La Pasiega, Puente Viesgo. Two small horses and fragment of a third.
	40	Rock engraving, La Pasiega, Puente Viesgo. Bison.
	41	Animal head, Altamira. A natural projection in the rock has been used and only the eyes and nostrils have been painted.
	42	Palimpsest, Altamira. Top layer shows painting of a leaping horse; beneath it are engravings of a hind and part of a horse, and below them a black contour fragment of a bison's head.
	43	Polychrome painting, Altamira. Wild boar (⅔ actual size).
	*44	Polychrome painting, Altamira. Bison cow (½ actual size). Eye, ear, beard and part of the contour are engraved as well as painted.
	45	Polychrome painting, Altamira. Bison horns engraved (½ actual size).
	46	Rock engraving, Altamira. Stag and fragment of a hind.
	47	Finger drawing in clay, Altamira. Head of bull or bison.
	48	Painting, Altamira. Tectiform.

EASTERN SPAIN Levant style	49	Painting, Cueva de Civil, Albocacer. Bowman.
	50	Painting, Cueva de Civil, Albocacer. Bowman.
	51	Painting, Cueva de Civil, Albocacer. Two running bowmen.
	52	Painting, Caballos, Albocacer. Two bowmen running at high speed. The lower figure is badly weathered.
	53	Painting, Mars del Josep, Albocacer. Stag hunt. *See page 35.*
	54	Painting, Saltadora, Albocacer. Four running bowmen.
	55	Painting, Saltadora, Albocacer. Deer.
	56	Painting, Morello. Bow fight. This picture is in the same miniature style which we find in parts of the Libyan Desert.
	57	Examples of East Spanish and Libyan art showing similarity in style.
NORTH-WESTERN SPAIN	58	Rock engraving, Pedra das Ferraduras, Fentans. Stag, smaller animals, swords or daggers and phalli.
	59	Rock engraving, Laxe dos Homos, near Campo le Nero. Anthropomorphic figures (½ actual size).
	60	Rock engraving, San Jorge de Mogor. Labyrinth.
	61	Rock engraving, Laxe das Lebras, Montecello. Male and female quadrupeds, probably deer.
	62	Rock engraving, near Pontevedra. Stag, cups and rings.
	63	Rock engraving, near Pontevedra. Cups and rings.

LIBYAN
DESERT

64 Painting, Wadi Sora. Acrobats. It may be seen here that the "dotted line" was not invented by the picture editor of a modern tabloid newspaper.

65 Painting, Wadi Sora. Dancers. Note the swing and movement. The white flecks are not skirts but spots where the stone has crumbled away.

66 Painting, Wadi Sora. Running figure with headgear similar to that of the Egyptian Pharoahs.

67 Painting, Wadi Sora. Hand and three figures. Probably the symbolic representation of a religious belief. *See frontispiece.*

68 Painting, Wadi Sora. Four running figures, badly weathered.

69 Painting, Wadi Sora. A prehistoric St. Sebastian, probably the symbolic representation of a rite connected with the Libyan predecessor of the Egyptian god, Set. *See page 44.*

70 Painting, Wadi Sora. Worshippers behind a bull.

71 Examples of animal worship motif in prehistoric art.

72 Painting, Ain Dua. Cattle of a graceful stag-like species now extinct. Note exaggeration of the udder showing that these are not wild but domestic animals. Cattle could not exist in this region today. *See page 41.*

73 Painting, Khargur Tahl. Domestic scene, man, two women and child.

74 Painting, Khargur Tahl. Man and woman.

75 Painting, Khargur Tahl. Fragment of a giraffe.

76 Painting, Khargur Tahl. Human figure with animal mask.

Many of the paintings (not the engravings) of the Libyan Desert are similar in style to those of Eastern Spain, and it is thought that either the same or very closely related cultures were responsible for both.

LIBYAN
DESERT

77 Painting, Yerhauda. A row of men dancing behind a cow. In the background the fragments of three large giraffes.

78 Painting, Khargur Tahl. Two cows and two small bowmen.

*79 Painting, Khargur Tahl. A fight, apparently for possession of a bull. Note action and grouping.

80 Painting, Wadi Sora. The large figures are apparently dancing, the small ones swimming. This is the only known picture of swimmers in prehistoric art.

81 Rock engraving, Wadi Hamra. Giraffes and antelope.

82 Rock engraving, Wadi Hamra. Bull.

SAHARA
ATLAS

*83 Rock engraving, Jaschu Plateau. Lion, *en face*.

84 Rock engraving, Jaschu Plateau. Five elephants. This picture is directly below that of the lion (No. 83). The lion seems to be represented as the ruler of the other beasts, a parallel for which exists in the cave of Trois Frères in Southern France.

85 Rock engraving, El Korema. Row of wild horses.

86 Rock engraving, Bou Alem. Ram with winged sun between his horns. Traces of color were found on this picture, leading to the assumption that the inner surfaces of most of the large Sahara rock pictures were originally painted. Since they stand in the open and are exposed to wind and driving sand, it is natural that the colors have disappeared.

87 Rock engraving, Enfouss. Two fighting buffaloes (bubali antiqui). *See page 37*.

88 Rock engraving, Enfouss. Two lions, small game and an elephant.

89 Rock engraving, Ain Safsaf. Elephant protecting its young from the attack of a panther or lioness.

74

SAHARA ATLAS	90	Rock engraving, Wadi Itel. Actually a palimpsest. In the lower (older) layer are human figures and animals finely drawn; in the upper layer are crudely drawn gnus and a red buffalo.
	91	Rock engraving, Tiout. Woman holding up her hands, man shooting at an ostrich. It is still a custom among certain peoples for the wife at home to hold up her arms while her husband is out hunting to bring him luck.
	92	Rock engraving, Djebel Bes-Seba. Man worshipping a sun-ram. On the right animal-like Siamese twins.
	93	Rock engraving, Oued Cheria. Animals, spirals and other signs probably having to do with hunting magic.
	94	Rock engraving, Oued Cheria. Much the same subject as No. 93.
FEZZAN	95	Rock engraving, Tel Issaghen. Buffalo (bubalus antiquus).
	96	Rock engraving, Tel Issaghen. The Barth Group (see page 38). Bull, men with animal masks.
	97	Rock engraving, Tel Issaghen. Ram's head and antelopes. The stone on which the ram was engraved weathered badly and part of it broke away, leaving only the ram's head. In a later period some one came along and engraved the antelopes *in the break*. Note the difference in style between the younger and the older work.
	98	Rock engraving, Tel Issaghen. Probably a ceremony in connection with the launching of a boat. There is no water there now.
	99	Rock engraving, In Habeter. Two elephants apparently about to attack. Note articulated ears. *See page 13.*

FEZZAN   100   Rock engraving, In Habeter. Domestic cattle and what is probably a sun symbol. Herodotus relates that in the land of the Garamantae (Fezzan) the horns of the cattle curved so far forward that the beasts had to graze backwards, something which we can take with a grain of salt. The cattle in this engraving, however, are probably of the type he meant to describe.

101   Rock engraving, In Habeter. Ostriches and four figures similar to the Egyptian god, Bes.

102   Rock engraving, In Habeter. Wart hog.

103   Rock engraving, In Habeter. Herd of cattle.

104   Rock engraving, In Habeter. Bowman.

105   Rock engraving, In Habeter. Elephant with man on trunk. Stone face badly weathered.

*106   Rock engraving, In Habeter. Six ostriches in what is possibly the hunter's magic circle.

*107   Rock engraving, In Habeter. Two men with animal masks dragging home a slain rhinoceros. The men are probably magicians. *Site illustrated*.

*108   Rock engraving, In Habeter. Giraffe, symbolic circle and a fragment of two ostriches. *Site illustrated*.

109   Rock engraving, In Habeter. Crouching lion.

110   Rock engraving, In Habeter. Man with a donkey's mask driving what looks like a water buffalo.

111   Rock engraving, In Habeter. Four ostriches.

112   Rock engraving, In Habeter. Rhinoceros.

113   Rock engraving, In Habeter. Animal mask.

114   Rock engraving, In Habeter. Long-legged elephant. Mouth and tusks drawn incorrectly.

*115   Rock engraving, In Habeter. Elephant and two giraffes. *Site illustrated*.

FEZZAN	116	Painting, Tadjem, Tassili Mountains. Sign.
	117	Painting, Ersach, Tassili Mountains. Sign.
	118	Painting, Ersach, Tassili Mountains. Hunting scene.

SOUTH AFRICA	119	Painting, Inoro Cave. Antelopes and human figures.
Southern Rhodesia	120	Painting, Gutu District. Burial scene. *See page 46.*
	121	Painting, Matopo Hills. Landscape with figures.

122 Painting, Rusapi. Rain ceremony (½ actual size). *See page 47.*

123 Painting, Mandarellas, Rusawi Valley. Rain ceremony (⅕ actual size).

124 Painting, Mandarellas District. Landscape with figures.

125 Painting, Mandarellas District. Seated figure.

126 Painting, Mandarellas District. Seated figure, birds.

127 Painting, Rusape. Burial scene. *See page 47.*

128 Painting, Lionshead, north of Salisbury. Slain animal (compare with No. 127).

129 Painting, Rusape. Burial scene (½ actual size). *See page 48.*

*130 Painting, Makumba Cave, Chinamora Reserve. Group of large formlings.

131 Painting, Mrewa. Formlings and figure.

132 Painting, Bindura. Bulbous growths, armed figure, buck and apes.

*133 Painting, Mtoko Cave. Large elephants, quagga, antelopes, formlings and figures.

134 Painting, Macheke. Three crouching figures.

135 Painting, Matopo Hills. Ape-like figure.

SOUTH AFRICA Southern Rhodesia	136	Painting, Mrewa. Fabulous animal (½ actual size).
	137	Painting, Macheke. Legless figures, animal heads.
	138	Painting, Salisbury. Long-legged figures, some with tails and animal heads.
	139	Painting, Makowe Cave. Two men, baboon, small buck, plants and flowers. Black and white figures like these are extremely rare.
	140	Painting, Massimbura, Chinamora Reserve. Long-legged dancers.
South African Union	141	Painting, Witzieshoek, Orange Free State. White figures with bird heads.
	142	Painting, Wepener Farm, Orange Free State (near Basutoland border). Snake and antelopes.
	143	Painting, Wepener Farm, Orange Free State (near Basutoland border). Running eland.
	144	Painting, Teyateyaneng, Basutoland. Rain ceremony.
	*145	Painting, Khotsa Cave, Basutoland. Large eland and human figures.
	146	Painting, Cinyati Cave, Natal. Man with elephant head. *See page 49.*
	147	Painting, Sunday Falls River, Natal. Men in costumes, antelope.
	148	Painting, Tembuland, Cape Province. Four figures in masks and gowns.
	149	Plaster cast of an engraving, Clerksdorp, West Transvaal. Eland. (Original in Capetown Museum.)
	150	Plaster cast of an engraving, Schweizer Reneke, West Transvaal. Buffalo. (Original in Capetown Museum.)

SOUTH AFRICA	151	Plaster cast of an engraving, Vryburg, Bechuanaland. Elephant. (Original in Capetown Museum.)
South African Union	152	Plaster cast of engraving, Vryburg, Bechuanaland. Young kudu. (Original in Capetown Museum.)
Southwest Africa	153	Painting, Great Spitzkopjes. Stylized praying mantes. *See page 52.*
	154	Painting, Small Spitzkopjes. Lying figure on which four smaller figures are superimposed.
	155	Painting, Jochman Cave. Running figure. Compare with running figures from Eastern Spain, particularly No. 52.
	156	Painting, Zisab Ravine, Brandberg. Men and animals. Note the richly decorated bowman on the right. *See page 51.*
	*157	Painting, Naukluft. Hunting scene. The hunters were apparently after the small buck in the center of the picture when they were rudely disturbed by the rhinoceros. *Illustrated by photograph of actual site.*

THREE THOUSAND COPIES OF THIS CATALOG HAVE BEEN PRINTED

FOR THE TRUSTEES OF THE MUSEUM OF MODERN ART AT THE

SPIRAL PRESS, NEW YORK · WITH COLLOTYPE REPRODUCTIONS

BY THE MERIDEN GRAVURE COMPANY AND FRONTISPIECE IN

SIMILETONE OFFSET BY ZEESE-WILKINSON COMPANY, INC.